Love
and
Tears
Why Question It?

CRYSTAL

authorHOUSE®

AuthorHouse™
1663 Liberty Drive
Bloomington, IN 47403
www.authorhouse.com
Phone: 1 (800) 839-8640

Published by AuthorHouse 10/03/2017

ISBN: 978-1-5462-1007-8 (sc)
ISBN: 978-1-5462-1006-1 (e)

Print information available on the last page.

This book is printed on acid-free paper.

Contents

Love yourself all day every day.

You will receive the love you deserve
and what God has for you.

If everyone in the world did the same thing, and accepted and
cherished life and love, this world would be a great place to
leave to our children, grandchildren, and future generations.

Acknowledgments

Thank you to everyone who loves me for being me; accepts me for who I am, without trying to change me; and loves me without question.

Thank you to all my children for making me want to be my best; you make me proud, and you can do anything you set your mind to, just put God first.

Thank you to my wonderfully loving husband, who encouraged me to continue my education. Thank you for being the one that dreams big for the both of us. I read somewhere to pray God-size prayers, and the success of this book would be a pebble in a sea of what God has for us.

Love Never Left Behind

Past the time,
Love is blind—
Love is something never left behind.

Love has many places;
I hope you'll save a part—
That one special place inside your heart.

You say I don't show the way I feel,
But my love for you is so very real.

If the time comes that we can be together,
Which at this time seems to be never,

One thing will never pass in time—
Is the love that you have left behind.

Let's Make A Toast

To you, my love: let's make a toast.
To you, my love: you've hurt me to the best of your ability.

To you, my love: let's drink this wine.
To you, my love: it's time to move on and forget about the past.

To you, my love: let's stop wasting time.
To this love, little attention was paid.
Love could have changed things!

To you, my love: it's time to realize what we could have had.
We've shared good times, bad times, and a very sacred love.
To you, my love: we know it is true;
My love was all yours 'til now.

My love, let's make a toast.
Now the wine is gone; the glasses are
ready to be washed and put away.
Tomorrow is yet another day, and true
love is sure to pass this way.

Jewel

This, my box, sits upon a shelf,
very plain to see:
this box is very important to me.

Everything I love and care for,
everything I treasure, special and true,
is kept inside for me,
to be

Safe from all harm;
but could cause an alarm,
if I open it and see
that your picture's not there in front of me.

My Prayer

Dear Lord, this I pray:
that any time, night or day,
you'll give the homeless a place to stay;

that you bless these families, struggling
and working hard to make a living,
with great food to have this Thanksgiving;

that you help me and others understand
how to keep trying situations well in hand;

that you help my mother, who does her best—
it seems her life has been filled with tests.
Thanks for helping her to survive.
She is a *Survivor*—that she is.

Dear Lord, I pray that you watch over my
sister and brother and let them know
there is no other more Powerful,
Forgiving, Wonderful, or Wise.

I don't have to wonder,
for I know it's true:
there is no other who loves me as you do.

Dear Lord, this I pray:
I will remember all the blessings, if
nothing else, until my dying day.

Amen! Amen! Amen!

Shorter

I found out the hard way
Something to keep in mind—

Love and happiness last a short time,
And
Life, even shorter.

The Color Of My Skin

Not as white
As the newly fallen snow,
But darker;

Not as dark
As the night when the
Stars seem to shine,
But lighter—

Which is somewhere
In the middle,

The color of my skin!

Too Late

Apprehensively pondering,
Committing grand larceny,
A premeditated crime of another kind.
Skeptical?
No!

Pretentiously counting
Money not yet in hand,
Cautiously going over the plan.
Intolerable acts,
A push and a shove.
Retaliate?
Yes!

He blames another,
Consciously knowing
He fears deeply.
Impatiently awaiting an answer,
He hears nothing.

Becoming hysterical,
"Meet here at three," he says.
He's inexplicably late;
Amnesia sets in.
He takes on a melancholy attitude—it's too late.

Fate

White all around—
On the rooftops
And the ground.

Skeptical about the position—
Why do my thoughts condescend my every move?

Help the lady to her room?

He becomes hysterical;
Unable to remain placid,
He panics.

Only knowing a mundane world,
Say nothing but "Yes, ma'am," "No, ma'am,"
"No, sir," "Yes, sir"—
He's subjected to a life of unfairness.

Intolerable, such mimicry;
An inevitable fate awaits me,
Forever caught in a vortex of racism!

Do I Really Have To Choose?

Do I really have to choose? In making my choice, will I lose?
The one who loves me more, than anyone before?
I'm really confused!
They love and care for me, one more than the other—
When really, I'm looking to be with the guy who's right for me.
But how will I know?
One respects me, treats me like a queen. From
the beginning, I thought it was just a dream.
The other takes charge, acts like a man.
He does for me what no other can.
So whom shall I pick?
I can choose to be with one or the other; I
could have them both or chose another.
Whom shall I pick?
How will I know?
I'm really confused!
So whom shall I choose:
One, two, or three?

So Real

Trees so tall
As the grass is high.

Walking together,
Your hand in mine.
Avoiding that look
Into your dark brown eyes.

Long,
A walk in the park
To find a place to sit,
To share our thoughts,
To talk … yes, relate.
Hands so softly placed
Upon my face;
We hesitate.

I turned away.
No games should we play.
You turn
To hold me close.

Your heartbeat I feel.
Should we kiss?
We did! What I feel … is so real!

Learning The Hard Way

Learning the hard way—

Unhappy,
Really I am.

Friend
To count on, or not?

Sexually …
The only way you see me.

Lies
Men tell—
You deceived me.

Here
To be a pincushion for your penis,
I am not!

You and I—
It can never be.

I learned the hard way.

Suspended In Time

Sweet words,
Frequent calls,
Little notes—
How I adore!

Your strong touch,
Your sweet caress,
Creamy wetness—
My body shakes!

So powerful,
Your body,
My body,
Mixing—
Now intertwined.

The music plays,
Forever softly plays—
Suspended in time!

Young Girl

All alone in the world,
Not ever really getting
To know herself
And what a beautiful woman
She could become.

Men see this girl,
Alone and unsure,
Only out for themselves,
Only out to score;
She knows no better.

Young girl,
Coming of age,
Ready to be grown
And out on her own—
Becoming free,
Reassured,
Independent, more mature.
Snatched from the sky
Like an unborn baby from its mother's womb,
She cries.

Young girl,
On to becoming a mother—

Happy,
Depressed,
Looking forward to the best.

But not the man—
Or should I say, little boy—
Who helped create
A life, a little girl
Whom she loves so much.

Young girl,
Not so young anymore,
Out in the world,
Just as before.
No, not like before—
Few hopes,
Lots of dreams,
No self-esteem.
Wanting to be reassured
Someone loves her and cares; she finds
it in the eyes of her child.
Why did she choose this man? Or did this man choose her?

Could he be the key,
To the most beautiful life
She's so eager to see?

Or did she choose this man,
A man who could care less, or
No one who would care more
Than to make this girl
His personal whore.

Love & You

Love and you–
You make me happy and
Fill my heart with joy.

Christmas, Love, and you—
You fulfill my every desire, want, and need, and
I strive to do the same for you.
So as requested, your gift under the tree will be me.

Love and you—
You are the one that I've searched my whole life for, and
You are a very special person in my life—you are my love.

Christmastime or anytime without you,
My love, would be
Like spending an eternity in hell, alone and lost—
But
You've reassured me that I don't have to pay that cost.

Love and you—
You make me happy
And
Fill my heart with joy.
Spending the rest of my life with you—
I need nothing more.

Could U?

A dream last night I had of you
Made me reminisce a time or two—

Just wanted to know, could you?

Could you be the steaming hot water in my bathtub,
Relaxing me from my head down to my toes,
Caressing my body, moving over and around every part of me,
Like the water of an ocean, all over?

Could you be my dripping-wet
Soapy sponge,
Cleansing away the tension,

Massaging my body where I need, my eyes closed,
My G-spot caressed and wet?

Could you be my favorite bottle of wine,
Chilled to perfection,
Cool going down; however, warming
my body from the inside out?
Help me to unwind.

Your lips I can't wait to kiss.

The air moving over me,
Drying my body effortlessly.
I lay with my back to the sheets, hot red silk,
My legs slightly parted, displaying a
rose where I'd like to be kissed.

Could you make love to me,
Over and over for days on end, turn me out?

Hoarse is my voice from the screams of passion.
We try not to wake the neighbors.

A dream last night I had of you
Made me reminisce a time or two—

Just wanted to know,
Could you?

My Best Friend

Brown:
One of my favorite colors and one of my
favorite people … how I'm glad
I broke my rule on personal space—the
last time we met, a hug goodbye.

Never realizing it would be the last time I'd see
your face or hear your voice, we'd talk
about it all—life and love—you heard my every word.

We even had a few laughs, and at the
time I'm sure I needed that!

True love
you found, and I was so happy for you; she
gave you love, balance, and was your dream
come true, your gift before life's end.

For me,
You gave me insight, advice, encouraged me to
fight, even when it seemed all was a waste,
and he would never open his eyes to see my pain.

That embrace—that's what I'll remember most.
I smile, and my heart sings:
That was God!
I miss my best friend.

That Was It

The words of a young girl
Depressed,
Feeling alone and unsure, no place to belong:

Give it time,
Love,
And friends will accept you for being
you and give of themselves;
Encouragement
And
Support
Really make all the difference.

Don't give up!
Be strong!
Hold on!

Those words fall on deaf ears and a heavy heart,
I have nothing to give, she screams as
the tears rolls down her face.

They don't care to know the hurt and the pain that I feel.

What can you do for me?
What material things do you have?

That's all they see.

"You have so much more to offer!"

The encouraging words broke through.

The sharp silver knife was put away.

The weighted black gun was unloaded
and returned to its hiding place.
The pills returned to the shelf behind the sliding glass.

Now a young woman with
Hopes,
Dreams,
Determination;

Now stronger and able to see a brighter day ahead.

Absentee father, that was it.
Strength of a mother, that was it.
His Love saved me, and that was it.

Be My Girl

One approached me … he did, smooth as could be,
Question dangling in the air behind his hello,

"Be my girl?"

I walk forward, glancing back for just a moment,
there's just half a block behind me.

Another approached me, yes, he did … playful yet surreal,
Got me thinking *what the hell*,
As he said,

"Be my girl?"

A question quickly came to me,
"Is this a joke, a test to see what my response will really be?"
I shake my head … boys!

A brick wall called me to rest as I
pulled my knees to my chest.
My eyes roam the ground for answers;
My current destination placed on hold.

The third, he approached, timid, shy, and yet full of hope—
Which could be heard in his voice,

The words he spoke filled with pride, yet
my eyes never left the ground
As I heard,

"Be my girl?"

My answer of "No! I can't!" was short—no
sweetness to be found as he walked away.

Years passed.
In a conversation I found that the one time
my eyes never left the ground,
That timid, shy, hopeful pride, stole my heart,
And now I call him,

"My husband."

Express Your Love

Hurt and depressed, I sit here,
Wondering, *Alone, will I forever be?*

I look back on the times we shared;
The one thing that changed you and me was
the one thing I thought I'd never see.

To be me, to give love freely, that's all I need,
Someone who can let me be me.

Memories:
In a boat on the lake, waiting for the unknowing
to take the bait we set, my first time fishing.

Sitting out on the grassy green, watching the sun rise,
Then sat and watched the planes that fly
by—a relaxing moment in time,
That's what we shared.

Is that how you express your love?

Memories:
Of you being assertive, knowing what you
want and expecting nothing less,
Preparing with your own hands a seductive
dessert of fruits and cream;

It's the little things as my fingertips meet your lips.
Is that how you express your love?

Memories:
A walk in the park, the wind blows, my
dress I press against my thighs,

A smile we share and a wink—this moment captured in time
As the flash of your camera captures the twinkle of my eyes.

The seafood dinner we also shared:
Shrimps, oysters and claims—
The taste, to die for.

Is that how you express your love?

Memories:
A night out totally obliterated our good times,
For the drinks that you indulged in were more
than you or I could handle or bear.

Out of control, that's what you became.

I sacrificed myself for you,
Put myself in harm's way to save you from *you*.

Your arm around my neck too tight, I recall
The imprint on my arm from your bite,
A search for my keys on the night's road,
The broken windshield,
The broken door—
Thank God you didn't break me.

My fear for you turned to fear of you.
To correct your mistakes of your overindulgence in spirits,
My depleted account represents that which had to be replaced.
But what shall I do with my heart?

Freely I gave my love and my time, so please tell me,
Is that how you express your love?

You Deserve

Long conversations,
When hours pass you by and the moments are not missed.
Hugs and kisses, freely given,
That start and end your days.

Foot massages and back rubs,
After a long day at work and moonlit nights at play.

Romantic meals for two,
Rooms illuminated by candlelight,
Jasmine-scented flowers and gifts just because.

Hot passionate sessions,
Lovemaking at hand,
Scattered rose petals of pink across purple satin sheets,
Your favorite fragrances caressing the air.

A long walk in the park,
Your hand in his, exploring the park together.

To lie back in his arms,
Sharing your dreams and hopes.

That diamond ring which represents respect,
promises of love, and a partnership
With a man you call friend and husband.

So when will you believe and see,
You deserve all this and much, much more.

True!

About the Author

Crystal is a native Washingtonian, raised in Southeast, Washington, DC. Where she lived, the parents in the neighborhood looked out for all the children. Her neighborhood was rich with love and hope. Life's path led her to drop out of high school, work multiple jobs, be with the wrong boy, and have a beautiful child. However, the love of her mother and the love for her daughter put her back on the right path.

Crystal went back to school and received her high school diploma. Later in life, she met the love of her life, who pushed her to be her best self. She graduated from college with degrees in business and contract management.

Crystal is now making her dream come true through sharing her work with the world. The words she lives by are "Change Your World" and "My lemons make the best lemonade."